D1630070

SOUTHWARK AND DEPTFORD TRAMWAYS

Robert J Harley

MP Middleton Press

First published August 1994

ISBN 1 873793 38 3

© Middleton Press 1994

Design - Deborah Goodridge

Published by Middleton Press
Easebourne Lane
Midhurst
West Sussex
GU29 9AZ
Tel: (0730) 813169
(From 16 April 1995 - (01730) 813169)

Printed & bound by Biddles Ltd,
Guildford and Kings Lynn

CONTENTS

INTRODUCTION AND ACKNOWLEDGEMENTS

If there ever was a spiritual home for the LCC tramcar, then the streets of inner South London could stake a serious claim. In contrast to the LT trolleybuses which always seemed more at ease in the avenues of 1920s and 1930s suburbia, the roads radiating from the Elephant and Castle were home territory for the trams. In this and other volumes I have tried to recreate the life and times of some of the busiest tramway junctions and thoroughfares in the capital. Inevitably with a large amount of material available the geographical boundaries between the three inner South London books have been rather arbitrary, and there is an element of overlap in the photographic coverage. I hope the reader will enjoy the trip along many streets which have now been altered beyond recognition. Some areas pictured in this album can hardly be called photogenic, however, they have been included as an historical record before they were swept away by so called road improvements. I hesitate to say that the main highways have been improved since the departure of the trams; the congestion and traffic fumes indicate that the area has yet to receive a transport system equal to the one it lost in July 1952.

I am grateful to the many photographers who have contributed to this book, their names are recorded in the following pages. I welcome a newcomer to the team in the person of D.Trevor Rowe who like the "regulars" was out and about recording the declining tramway scene in the early 1950s. As usual I offer my thanks to the staff of the library at the National Tramway Museum which is a splendid resource for all seekers after knowledge in the tramway field. Material from the collection of the late Alan Watkins has been kindly loaned by Ann Watkins. Many of the maps used in this book are based on the excellent pioneer work of the late Frank Merton Atkins.

GEOGRAPHICAL SETTING

This region of London adjacent to the River Thames has been settled for many centuries and urban development has been continuous until modern times. Municipal parks provide the only green areas, although in the 1980s more open space has been released with the redevelopment of the former docklands. There are no appreciable gradients or hills in the locality.

HISTORICAL BACKGROUND

The south bank of the River Thames was formerly attached to the county of Surrey and the settlement of Southwark has many famous historical connections with Chaucer's pilgrims and the Globe Theatre where some of the greatest Shakespeare plays were first performed. The area around Marshalsea Prison features in Charles Dicken's "Little Dorrit" which was written in 1855-7. In the Victorian era a vaste expansion of housing to accommodate artisans and daily labourers occurred; this naturally resulted in a demand for cheap and reliable transport. Horse trams first appeared on the Old Kent Road in 1871 and the tracks were later extended across the Elephant and Castle junction towards St. George's Circus. The section along Walworth Road opened in the same year and direct lines from Kennington to the Elephant and along Great Dover Street to St. George's Church followed in 1874. These lines were all operated by the London Tramways Company. Another network of horse lines sprang up in 1880-2 and

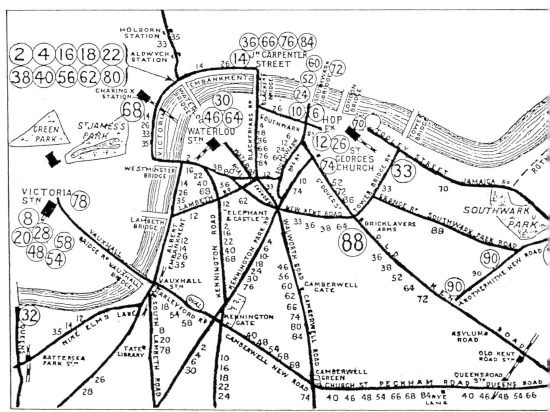

rails were laid by the London, Deptford and Greenwich Tramways Company from Deptford Noah's Ark to Tooley Street with branches along Rotherhithe New Road, Grange Road, Spa Road and Bermondsey New Road to the Bricklayers Arms. Yet another concern, the South London Tramways Company constructed tracks in 1883 through the Borough along Southwark Bridge Road to a terminus at Hop Exchange, not far from London Bridge station. There matters rested until the formation of the London County Council at the end of the nineteenth century.

The reconstruction of all horse tramways for electric traction on the conduit system was pursued with some vigour by the council and although the LCC was constantly thwarted by powerful "City" interests which were hostile to what they regarded as a "proletarian" mode of transport, a number of new electric lines were inaugurated to cover gaps in the former horse car network. Most of the new electric tracks around the Elephant and Castle were carrying passengers by the end of 1904; the western end of Southwark Street opened in 1909. It could

be said that the area immediately north of the Elephant was overprovided with electric tramways and although in later years it was useful to have alternative routes to use as diversions, some of the new lines became mere backwaters in the capital's transport system. The service from Tooley Street to Greenwich was converted in stages and, with the rebuilding of Creek Bridge for trams in October 1912 and a short extension by London Bridge station in December 1912, the electrification work was completed. The Tooley Street line was the subject of two experiments by the LCC tramways; from May to December 1913 a couple of petrol electric cars were tested and, in the period 1915-24, trailer cars were operated on the service. In 1913 the horse car service 90 along Rotherhithe New Road was withdrawn and two years later the LCC finally closed the horse era when service 88 along Grange Road and Southwark Park Road was abandoned. The final tramway extension in the area took place in July 1925, when double track was opened across Southwark Bridge to a new terminus at the junction of Queen Street and Upper Thames Street.

During the inter-war years, the trams carried large numbers of passengers and cars were improved with faster motors and more comfortable seats. The formation of the London Passenger Transport Board in 1933 put a question mark over further tramway development and some months later the first plans were announced for the conversion of the system to trolleybuses. No doubt, one of the contributing factors to the downfall of the tram was the high cost of the conduit system as opposed to the more conventional overhead wire method of current collection. Surveys were conducted by London Transport for the implementation of the new trolleybus routes throughout this area of South London, but the conversion programme came to a halt with the Second World War and in 1946 LT announced that motor buses would be used instead of trolleybuses to replace the remaining trams. The sad process of withdrawing services in Southwark and Deptford began in September 1950 and ceased with the final closure of the London system in July 1952.

London County Council Tramways

QSP = QUEEN ST. PLACE
SB = SOUTHWARK BRIDGE   ✳ = HOP EXCHANGE

CANNON STREET STN.

QSP

SB

CITY OF LONDON
STEPNEY

THE TOWER

ORIGINAL TERMINUS UNTIL 1925

LONDON BRIDGE

ST. KATHERINE DOCKS

SOUTHWARK

ROAD

STR.

HAY'S WHARF

TOWER BRIDGE

WAPPING STN.

SOUTHWARK BDG.

MARSHALSEA ROAD

HIGH STREET

LONDON BRIDGE STN.

TOOLEY

THE...

ST. SAVIOUR'S DOCK

BERMONDSEY STREET

ST. SAVIOUR'S DOCK

BOROUGH STN.

ST. GEORGE'S CHURCH

BERMONDSEY

STREET ROAD

DOCKHEAD

BOROUGH

BOROUGH ROAD

BERMONDSEY

GREAT DOVER ST.

BRIDGE

PARKERS ROW

JAMAICA

ROAD

GROVE

ELLSL

DRUMMOND RD.

LS

LS = LANCASTER STR.

NC = NEWINGTON CAUSEWAY

ABBEY ST.

SPA ROAD

TOWER

NC

▲ = ELEPHANT AND CASTLE P.H.

GRANGE

ROAD

NEW KENT ROAD

BRICKLAYERS ARMS

BRICKLAYERS ARMS GOODS STN.

SOUTHWARK

PARK RD.

RAYMO

ELEPHANT + CASTLE STN.

OLD

WALWORTH RD.

KENT RD.

EAST STREET

BERMONDSEY

NEW

PENROSE STR.
LONDON TRAMWAY CO's DEPOT & WORKS
(HORSE CARS)

ROTHERHITHE

WESTMORELAND ROAD

SOUTHWARK

CAMBERWELL

ALBANY ROAD

SURREY CANAL

BOWLES ROAD

OLD KENT RD

CAMBERWELL ROAD

SCALE

0   1 KM.

0   1/8   1/4   1/2
ONE HALF MILE

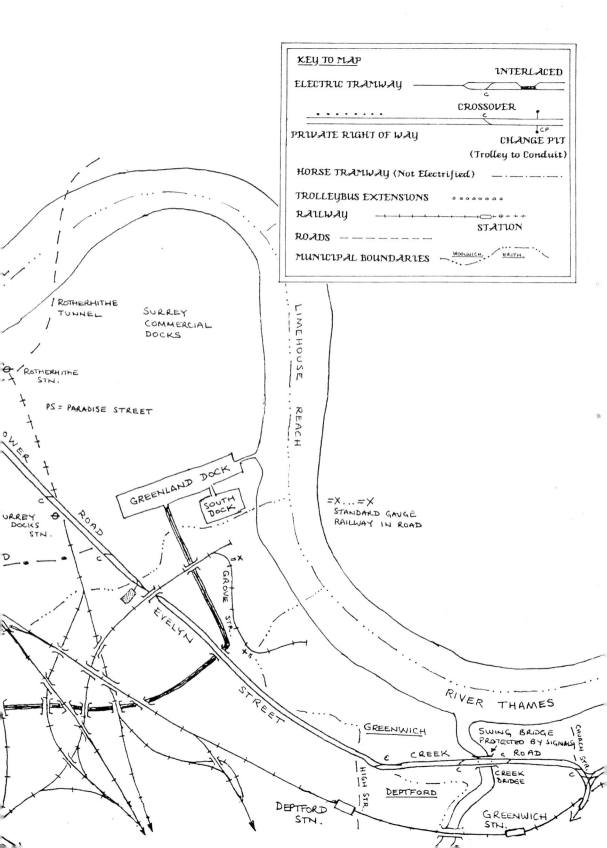

KEY TO MAP

ELECTRIC TRAMWAY — INTERLACED

CROSSOVER

PRIVATE RIGHT OF WAY · · · · · · · ·

CHANGE PIT (Trolley to Conduit)

HORSE TRAMWAY (Not Electrified) —··—··—··—

TROLLEYBUS EXTENSIONS ooooooo

RAILWAY —+—+—+—+— STATION

ROADS — — — — —

MUNICIPAL BOUNDARIES ·WOOLWICH· ··ERITH··

ROTHERHITHE TUNNEL

SURREY COMMERCIAL DOCKS

LIMEHOUSE REACH

ROTHERHITHE STN.

PS = PARADISE STREET

GREENLAND DOCK

SOUTH DOCK

=X ...=X STANDARD GAUGE RAILWAY IN ROAD

ROAD

SURREY DOCKS STN.

GROVE STR.

EVELYN STREET

RIVER THAMES

GREENWICH

SWING BRIDGE PROTECTED BY SIGNALS

CHURCH STR.

CREEK

ROAD

HIGH STR.

CREEK BRIDGE

DEPTFORD

GREENWICH STN.

DEPTFORD STN.

1. Approaches to Southwark Bridge and Hop Exchange

1.   Bright sunshine shone on the last day of tramway operation in the capital, 5th July 1952. Former West Ham car 295 waits to depart Southwark Bridge on a final journey to New Cross depot. Note the temporary ramps in the roadway behind the tram; these were constructed to enable traffic to cross bomb damage.   (National Tramway Museum. R.B.Parr)

2. Groups of City workers assemble to board their car home after a day at the office. The two cars on service 48 were both rehabilitated by LT in the 1930s; this rebuilding scheme probably prolonged the life of some trams as well as making them more comfortable for the travelling public. (D.Trevor Rowe Coll.)

3. Car 1145 brings up the rear of a line of trams waiting to reverse at the northern end of Southwark Bridge. Note that the conduit slot rails are positioned off centre between the tracks. (D.A.Thompson)

4. Looking towards the north west, we espy two trams of different parentage. The leading car was constructed by East Ham Corporation very much on traditional lines. The tram behind is a class UCC Feltham car built for the MET and LUT companies to combat motor bus competition; they were comfortable and modern trams. (A.J.Watkins)

5. The date is 1st October 1950 and car 1930 on service 10 bides its time until car 1606 on service 46 leaves the terminal stub for the return journey to Woolwich via Eltham. (R.J.S.Wiseman)

6. Time has moved on to June 1952, a slight haze has settled on the south bank of the Thames, a tramway replacement RT type diesel bus is spotted in the distance and a service 46 tramcar stands in splendid isolation as the power station chimney nears completion. (R.J.S.Wiseman)

7. The dome of St. Paul's rises above the City of London as a tram and bus are about to pass on Southwark Bridge. On 14th July 1925, the Lord Mayor of London, Sir Alfred Bowyer drove the first tram, car 1847, across the rebuilt bridge and the LCC gained another precarious foothold in the City. (J.H.Price Coll.)

8. Not long before the end of tramway operation, car 1855 rumbles towards the crossover near Sumner Street at the southern approach to the bridge. (D.A.Thompson)

9. The junction of Southwark Bridge Road with Southwark Street sees car 1422 clattering over the crossing outside the Metropolitan public house, in the summer of 1949 . At weekday peak times around 140 trams per hour would pass this spot. (D.A.Thompson)

10. Further along Southwark Street, car 208 is operating on service 26 whose journey time betwen Clapham Junction and London Bridge, (Borough Hop Exchange) was calculated at 41 minutes. The interval between trams on the full service was 10-15 minutes. (John H.Meredith)

11. The tracks from Southwark Street joined those in Blackfriars Road just south of Blackfriars Bridge. Car 1766, outbound on service 26, is about to head north to cross the bridge and run along the Victoria Embankment. This section is covered fully in the companion Middleton Press volume, *Embankment and Waterloo Tramways*. (John H.Meredith)

12. We retrace our steps in time to witness the arrival of a service 12 car at the Hop Exchange terminus situated in the Borough near to London Bridge station. Don Thompson, the photographer, seems to be the only soul about on this June day in 1949; this is in stark contrast to the usual congested scene of costermongers' barrows, horse drawn carts, lorries and crates of farm produce which obstructed the highway at market time during the week. (D.A.Thompson)

13. The end of the track at Hop Exchange is seen with a little more activity than the previous view. That the line ended here and was not permitted to join the Tooley Street terminus of service 70 just round the corner, was a source of frustration for the LCC. Needless to say, when buses replaced trams they were not inhibited by these rather pointless geographical restrictions. (A.J.Watkins)

14.   One of the shortest lived tram service extensions was instituted in October 1950 when, with the demise of services 12 and 26, service 72 was prolonged from Savoy Street to cover the otherwise tramless tracks. One presumes that LT wasn't quite ready to take the plunge and leave this section totally at the mercy of the central bus department! Whatever the reason, the Indian summer of the 72s lasted only a few months and in July 1951 the Borough terminus fell silent for ever. (C.Carter)

15.   The motorman of car 2055 rests his arm on the headlamp mask which was first fitted to comply with blackout regulations during the war. London Transport never got round to removing them after hostilities had ceased. (A.J.Watkins Coll.)

16. Back at Southwark Bridge Road a service 12 tram turns into Southwark Street whilst a following Feltham type car waits to proceed straight across the junction. (R.J.S.Wiseman)

17. Many readers will remember the 1950s Post Office Telephones vans, one of which halts at the lights in Southwark Bridge Road. Behind the tram a notice advertises car garaging at one shilling and sixpence (7p) a day; for the same priviledge today, the cost is over 300 times more expensive! (R.J.S.Wiseman)

18. A Southern Region suburban electric train thunders above car 342 which is making its own, somewhat more sedate, way towards the suburbs. Note the tram stop with accompanying passenger shelter. The bridge replaced one destroyed by enemy action in April 1941. (C.Carter)

⟶

20. The red flags and wheelbarrow indicate track repairs near the junction with Union Street. (John H.Meredith)

19. A solemn occasion on 5th January 1952 and the last ever service 52 car halts on Southwark Bridge Road for a commemorative photograph. (R.J.S.Wiseman)

⟶

21. Gloomy weather conditions in November 1951 seem to fit the surroundings as car 994 on service 52 just edges ahead of the competition at the junction of Marshalsea Road. (D.Trevor Rowe)

22.   At the corner of Great Suffolk Street and
Southwark Bridge Road car 210 waits for the
lights to change. The green light had already
been given for bus conversion and the
temporary tram stop sign presages an
imminent increase in diesel fumes along this
street.   (John H.Meredith)

23.   Swinging into Borough Road car 202
continues its journey to Wandsworth.
(John H.Meredith)

24.   We pull back from the railway bridge in
the previous photo to look east along Borough
Road with the junction with Lancaster Street
in the foreground.   (D.A.Thompson)

25. It is September 1950 and the famous music hall star, George Robey is billed to appear at the Palace, Camberwell. Like the trams, the days were numbered for this particular form of entertainment. Note the splayed tracks here at the western end of Borough Road just before St. George's Circus and the splendid Guy lorry with its cargo of Lyons swiss rolls. (John H.Meredith)

27. Car 1892 is in Borough High Street at the junction with Borough Road. (John H.Meredith)

←

26. In peak hours when the approach along London Road to the Elephant was congested with trams, a southbound diversion operated from St. George's Circus via Borough Road, Lancaster Street, Southwark Bridge Road and Newington Causeway. Here we see one of the last service 34 cars to use this route; the date is 30th September 1950 and car 1384 is about to turn from Southwark Bridge Road into Newington Causeway. (John H.Meredith)

28. At the same junction as in the previous photo, a service 48 car loads, as the lorry behind the tram is forced to take avoiding action. (R.J.S.Wiseman)

29.   Pictured here at the eastern end of Borough Road is the LT quarterly car which ran over these otherwise unused tracks to maintain London Transport's legal ownership rights. According to law if no tram operated over a particular section of track for three months then the local authority could require the operator to remove said tracks. Happily there is no one waiting at the stop for the next car along in ninety days time!
(D.A.Thompson)

2. Elephant and Castle

30.   Six major roads all bearing tramways converged at the Elephant and Castle, so named after the public house which stood on one corner of the junction. An animated scene greets us as we look towards Newington Causeway. (R.J.Harley Coll.)

Horse tramway layout in 1895 at 50" to 1 mile.

31.   In horse car days the layout was only slightly less elaborate. Note the rather outlandish touch of the three mules pulling the horse tram past the original Elephant and Castle. (A.J.Watkins Coll.)

Oil & Co&
Warehouse

PRINCESS PLACE

PRINCESS MEWS

Parliamentary Bo

T R

P.H.

H

Drinking
Fountain

F P

P.H.

T
R

Urinal

P.H.

P.H.

F P

H

Warehouse

Bank

Stores

L.B.

F.P.

M.S

Elephant &
Castle
P.H.

SHORT
STREET

Station

P.O.

P.H.

H

T
E
M
P
L
E
S
T
R
E
E
T

L.B.

b.s

H

P.H.

Smithy

P.H.

H

B.P.

I.F.W.

I.F.W.

F.W.

B.P.

F.W.

Metropolitan Tabernacle
(Baptist)
Seats for 5600

Bank

11·8

B.Ps

Boys & Girls

F.W.

F.P

H

Carriage Manufactory

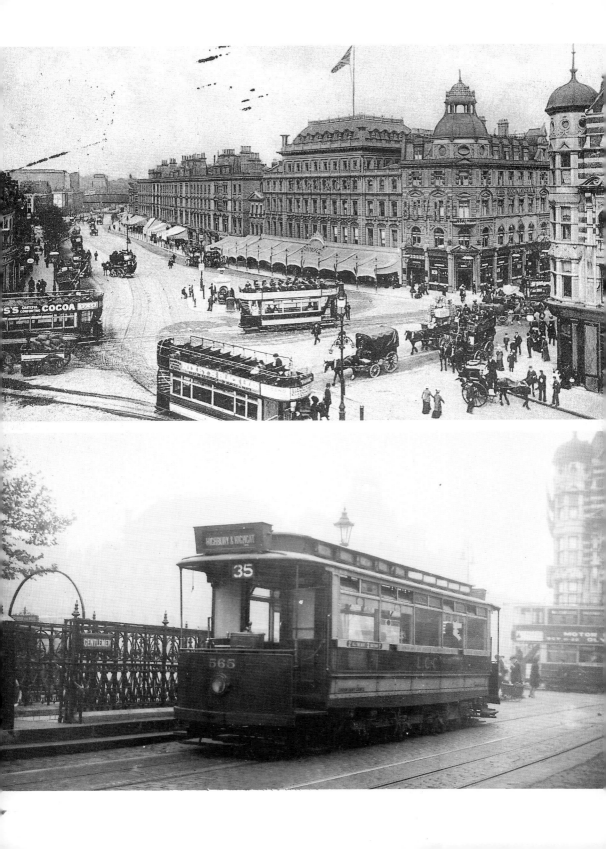

32.   Very early in the electric era a three window, four wheel car scuttles across the junction about to pass the Rockingham Arms and out into the New Kent Road. The larger bogie car at the bottom of the picture is turning from Newington Butts into London Road. (J.H.Price Coll.)

34. A carter guides his horse in the direction of Walworth Road; in the opposite direction the motorman of the service 6 car will hold his course heading for Newington Causeway and Southwark Bridge. (J.H.Price Coll.)

33. Car 565, one of the vehicles built to run through the Kingsway tram subway, waits in the entrance to St. George's Road before reversing and setting off on the return journey to Highgate. An illustrated account of the Kingsway subway appears in the companion volume *Embankment and Waterloo Tramways*. (G.N.Southerden)

←

35.   Not every visitor to the Elephant in pre-LT days bore the familiar colours of the London County Council. An Embankment bound Croydon Corporation car pulls up to let a rather careless pedestrian saunter over the tracks. (G.N.Southerden)

←

36. Fred Upton's the hatter has been replaced by the Burton building and the other vacant lots in this post war view are courtesy of the Luftwaffe; this part of London suffered quite heavily in the war. Note the group of painters and decorators off to the next job, no smart vans or mobile phones in those days! (D.A.Thompson)

37.   A fine summer's day in June 1912 sees plenty of activity. A tram with New Coss Gate via Peckham on its destination blind follows the single track along the eastern side of the Elephant and Castle public house which will then lead into Walworth Road. Note that although the double deck tram has a trolley hook attached to the edge of the roof, the trolley boom has yet to be fitted to the car. (R.J.Harley Coll.)

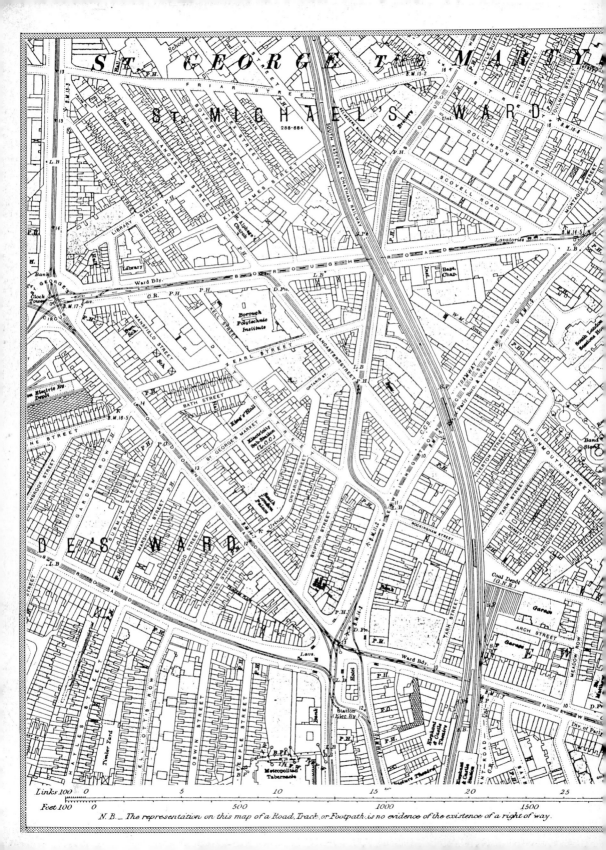

38. Almost the same location as the picture
before, this time 22 years of transport progress
have been made. A line of trams emerges from
London Road to confront an assortment of
motor buses. (A.J.Watkins Coll.)

39. Many tram drivers maintained that the
police controlled traffic lights were more of a
hindrance than a help. The traffic seems to be
flowing smoothly as car 192 forms part of a bus
sandwich. (D.A.Thompson)

40. What is now the Bakerloo line of the Underground reached the Elephant and Castle in August 1906; outside the entrance to the station in London Road passengers wait to make the change to the LCC trams. (R.J.Harley Coll.)

41. A policeman stands at the corner of Newington Causeway and London Road as a succession of trams passes the tube station with the offices of the South London Press above. The papers provided the only forum for debate about the tram scrapping question; the powers that be had already made up their minds. (John H.Meredith)

42. The bus and green line coach stop informs travellers of their exact whereabouts; car 169 approaches along St. George's Road. (D.A.Thompson)

43. Newington Butts and yet another very informative bus stop. After the trams were abandoned the whole junction was remodelled to incorporate a large roundabout surrounding an appalling box structure supported by slabs looking like concrete waffles. (D.A.Thompson)

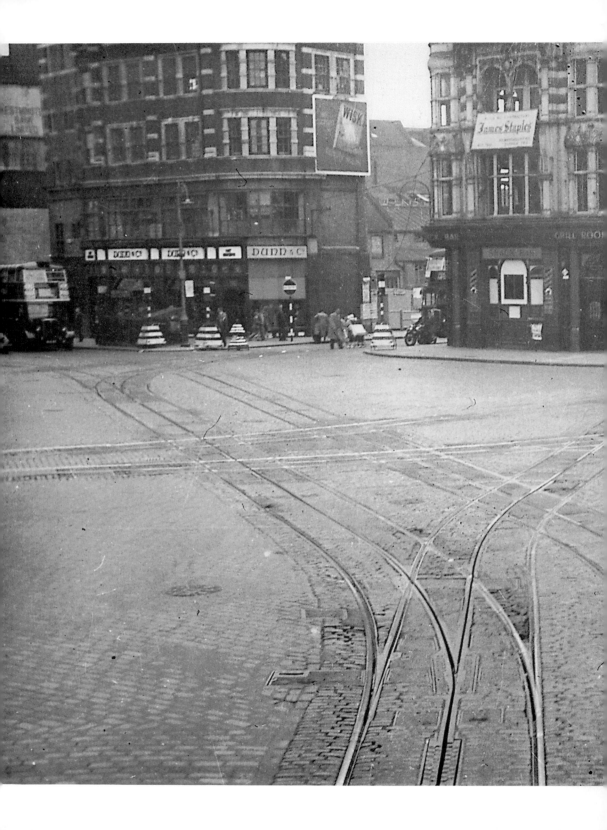

44. Taken from the top deck of a car in London Road, this view gives a good idea of the complexity of the junction. Worthy of note is the single track curve leading to Walworth Road which passes through the gap between the Elephant and Castle public house and the Dunn & Co. building. On the right of this view can be seen the dome of the old Northern Line tube station. (National Tramway Museum/ H.B.Priestley)

45.   The official title of the road outside the tube station was Short Street; car 1913 is caught by the camera on its long haul to North London.   (D.Trevor Rowe)

46.   Car 1858 on service 56 was later saved from the scrap heap and is now running at the East Anglian Transport Museum. An LT inspector looks on as a service 34 car wilfully disobeys the No Entry sign! (A.J.Watkins Coll.)

47. Another view of a tram running against the traffic flow. One can only assume that the road planners weren't prepared to wait for the abandonment of the trams before indulging in this highly dangerous practice; of course no funds were forthcoming from LT to modernise the tram tracks. It goes without saying that the money was found to raze the buildings and remodel the whole highway network at the Elephant in the 1950s and 60s. (D.A.Thompson)

48. Almost 3.45 pm on the famous illuminated Guinness clock and a service 38 car accelerates towards New Kent Road. (D.Trevor Rowe)

49. With the Trocadero left behind on the Elephant side of the bridge, car 554 leads the procession of a Green Line coach and a couple of buses out along the New Kent Road. The temporary open space to the right of the tram was caused by the wartime bombing. (D.A.Thompson)

3. Walworth Road

50.   Open platforms were the norm for most London tramcars as is illustrated in this view at the northern end of Walworth Road. The Metropolitan Police objected to the motorman standing behind a protective windscreen and the rule was only relaxed in the 1930s long after most other British cities had all enclosed cars. (G.N.Southerden)

51. A lone policeman directs the crowds back as HM King Edward VII is about to pass on his way to lay the foundation stone of King's College Hospital in July 1909. Outside the Red Lion, Camberwell Gate, LCC car 97 acts as a grandstand. (National Tramway Museum)

52. Pedestrians mill about on Walworth Road near a bakery advertising its wares. Also in this neck of the woods was a cafe with a notice proclaiming "Come on in - before we both starve." (D.Trevor Rowe)

53. The end of our coverage in this section brings us to Camberwell Green, pictured here a few years before the First World War. Further views of this location appear in companion volume, *Camberwell and West Norwood Tramways*. (National Tramway Museum)

4. St. George's Church

54. Borough High Street and car 170 sets off for West Norwood as RT 2025 loads at the bus stop; route 95 took over from tram service 10 on 7th January 1951. In the background is the Parish Church of St. George The Martyr, built in 1734-6 by John Price on the site of a medieval church. (D.Trevor Rowe)

56. Was the tram the cause of the traffic holdup outside the church, or was it being impeded by badly positioned motor vehicles? (Lens of Sutton)

55. The first tube station at the Borough opened with the City and South London Railway in 1890; it took another fourteen years for further electric traction in the shape of the LCC tramways to arrive at the door. With our backs to St. George's Church we witness the LT quarterly car slowly gouging out the mud from the rail grooves it inches its way round the disused curve from Great Dover Street to Borough High Street. (D.A.Thompson)

57. Car 1932 travels along Great Dover Street. Although some of the property hereabouts had seen better days, the afternoon sunshine picks out a pleasant terrace of houses, each with front railings which somehow escaped the melting pot during the wartime scrap metal drives. (D.A.Thompson)

58. On 8th September 1951 car 304 slows for the tram stop on Great Dover Street. Already there is evidence of the massive rebuilding programme to repair the destruction of the blitz. (R.J.S.Wiseman)

5. Bricklayers Arms and the Old Kent Road

59. The crossroads at the Bricklayers Arms is named after the public house opposite the library seen here at the corner of Great Dover Street and the New Kent Road. This and the following photos give some idea of the roads and the buildings before they were all demolished to make way for a flyover and a large roundabout. (D.Trevor Rowe)

60. The last day of trams in London and car 187 waits for some Saturday shoppers before proceeding southwards into the Old Kent Road. (R.J.S.Wiseman)

61. The tramways in central London often had to pass either side of public conveniences situated in the middle of the highway. Car 165, again on the last day, halts outside the gents; note the Bricklayers Arms pub in the background. (National Tramway Museum/ R.B.Parr)

62. Looking down along Tower Bridge Road, a service 68 car crosses on the way to Waterloo station. Parked on the left hand side is an LT repair wagon bearing a rather superfluous warning about overhead repairs. The nearest wires were across the river in trolleybus territory. (D.A.Thompson)

63. Trams and the Old Kent Road belonged together right from the very first horse car in July 1871 to the last electric tram in July 1952. The Castle public house basks in the sunshine whilst car 578 clatters along outside. Note George Carter and Sons emporium with its famous clock where the hat was raised on the striking of the hour. (D.A.Thompson)

64. Like many other thoroughfares in South London, the Old Kent Road was once lined with a multitude of colourfully named inns. The Dun Cow stands out on the left of the picture; in addition to the usual ales and spirits it offers, as the white post proclaims, luncheons. On the tramway scene car 1619 is short working to Bricklayers Arms. (D.A.Thompson)

65. The ruined shell of the public baths building by Marlborough Grove is awaiting reconstruction and behind the photographer a bomb site had been cleared by London Transport and was used as a permanent way yard for storing rails and paving materials. (D.A.Thompson)

66. Another view of the public baths was taken not long after the electric tramway opened in January 1904. Car 350 is about to cross the entrance to Bowles Road by the Lord Wellington pub. A former horse car depot was in use at the end of Bowles Road from 1874 until the conversion to electric traction in 1904; this was a short lived arrangement and when New Cross opened in 1905, the building was vacated and sold to the London General Omnibus Company. Its role as a bus garage ceased in November 1958. (R.J.Harley Coll.)

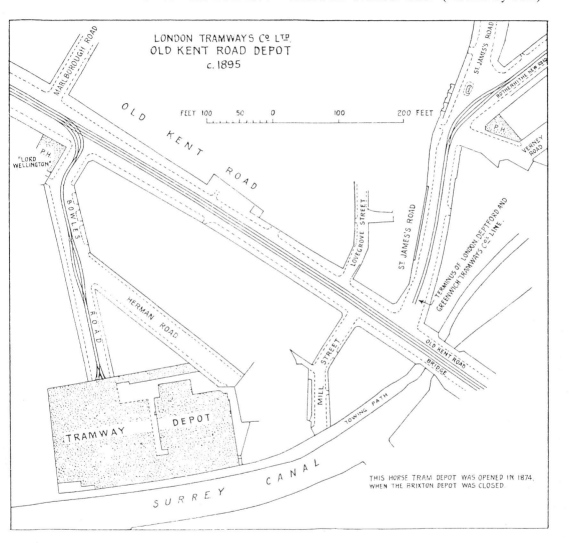

LONDON TRAMWAYS Cº LTº.
OLD KENT ROAD DEPOT
c. 1895

FEET 100   50   0   100   200 FEET

THIS HORSE TRAM DEPOT WAS OPENED IN 1874, WHEN THE BRIXTON DEPOT WAS CLOSED.

67. Those silent film buffs who know the Harold Lloyd classic "Speedy" will immediately recognise the scenario of the outdated horse car service plodding on against all adversity. Here is the "ha'penny bumper" eking out its last days; this line was never electrified and in 1911 it was timed at 7 minutes for the journey from Raymouth Road to St.James Road, terminus depicted here. (R.J.Harley Coll.)

68. There are plenty of period vehicles about in this Old Kent Road scene near the corner of Asylum Road. (R.J.S.Wiseman)

69. The motorman has placed the chain across the driving platform to discourage any unauthorised boarding. In fact, it was quite common for passengers carrying heavy sacks or flower baskets on the way to market to come round the front end and stow the goods next to the driver, thus further demonstrating the tramcar's versatility. (R.J.S.Wiseman)

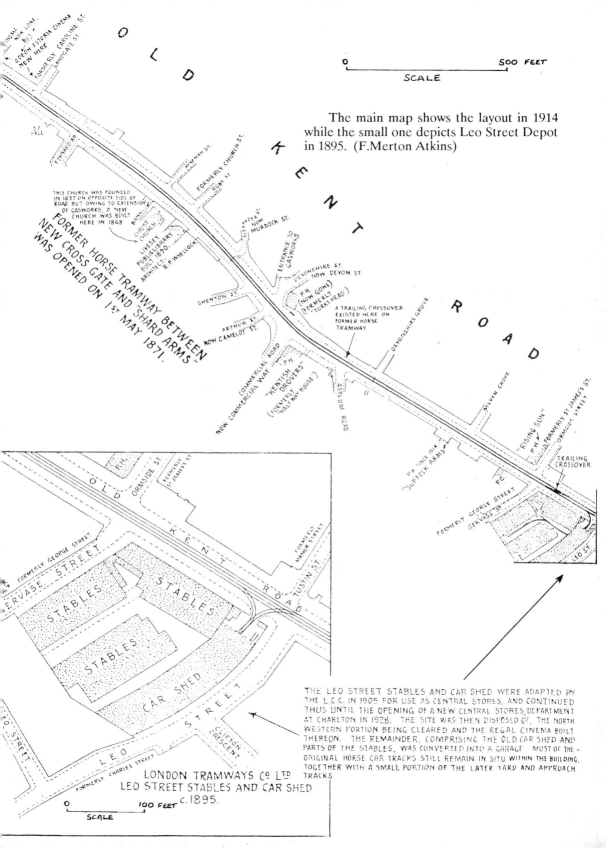

The main map shows the layout in 1914 while the small one depicts Leo Street Depot in 1895. (F.Merton Atkins)

O L D   K E N T   R O A D

CINEMA NOW GONE, BUT
ODEON ASTORIA CINEMA
NEW HERE
FORMERLY CAROLINE ST.
SANDGATE ST.

51 HALL

EDWARD RD

FORMERLY CHURCH ST.
FORMERLY ST.
RUBY ST.

THIS CHURCH WAS FOUNDED
IN 1837 ON OPPOSITE SIDE OF
ROAD BUT OWING TO EXTENSION
OF GASWORKS, A NEW
CHURCH WAS BUILT
HERE IN 1868

CHRIST CHURCH

LIVESEY
PUBLIC LIBRARY
BUILT 1890.
ARCHITECT R.P.WHELLOCK

NOW MURDOCK ST.

ENTRANCE TO GASWORKS

DEVONSHIRE ST.
NOW DEVON ST.

SHENTON ST.

P.H.
(NOW GONE)
(FORMERLY
TURKS HEAD)

A TRAILING CROSSOVER
EXISTED HERE ON
FORMER HORSE
TRAMWAY

ARTHUR ST.
NOW CAMELOT ST.

DEVONSHIRE GROVE

FORMER HORSE TRAMWAY BETWEEN
NEW CROSS GATE AND "SHARD ARMS".
WAS OPENED ON 1ST MAY 1871.

NOW COMMERCIAL ROAD
COMMERCIAL WAY

P.H.
"KENTISH
DROVERS"
(FORMERLY
"HALF WAY HOUSE")

ASYLUM ROAD

SYLVAN GROVE

"RISING SUN"
P.H.
FORMERLY ST JAMES'S ST.
ORMSIDE STREET

TRAILING
CROSSOVER

P.H. SINCE 1914
"SUFFOLK ARMS"

P.O.

FORMERLY GEORGE STREET
GERVASE ST.

LEO ST.

SCALE   0 ___ 500 FEET

OLD ORMSIDE ST.
FORMERLY ST. JAMES ST.
TUSTIN ST.

P.H.

O L D   K E N T   R O A D

FORMERLY NANGA STREET

FORMERLY GEORGE STREET
GERVASE STREET

STABLES
STABLES
STABLES

CAR SHED

LEO   STREET

CLIFTON
CRESCENT

LEO STREET

FORMERLY CHARLES STREET

LONDON TRAMWAYS Cº LTD
LEO STREET STABLES AND CAR SHED c.1895.

SCALE   0 ___ 100 FEET

THE LEO STREET STABLES AND CAR SHED WERE ADAPTED BY
THE L.C.C. IN 1905 FOR USE AS CENTRAL STORES, AND CONTINUED
THUS UNTIL THE OPENING OF A NEW CENTRAL STORES DEPARTMENT
AT CHARLTON IN 1928. THE SITE WAS THEN DISPOSED OF, THE NORTH
WESTERN PORTION BEING CLEARED AND THE REGAL CINEMA BUILT
THEREON. THE REMAINDER, COMPRISING THE OLD CAR SHED AND
PARTS OF THE STABLES, WAS CONVERTED INTO A GARAGE. MOST OF THE
ORIGINAL HORSE CAR TRACKS STILL REMAIN IN SITU WITHIN THE BUILDING,
TOGETHER WITH A SMALL PORTION OF THE LATER YARD AND APPROACH
TRACKS

70. A modern tramway system should play a major part in getting the capital moving again and it is to be hoped that this part of London may again see rails along the streets. For now we bid farewell with this photo of car 166. The first generation of tramcars served the Old Kent Road and its inhabitants so well for many years. (D.A.Thompson)

6. Tower Bridge Road

71. The bridge carrying the main railway line to central London spans Tower Bridge Road at the junction with Church Street. (D.A.Thompson)

Tooley Street and Old Kent Road to Deptford (Electric and Horse Traction).

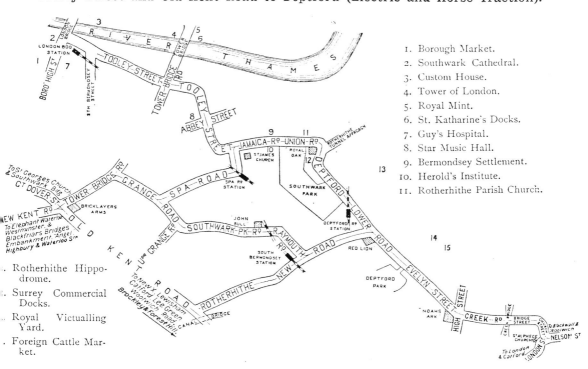

1. Borough Market.
2. Southwark Cathedral.
3. Custom House.
4. Tower of London.
5. Royal Mint.
6. St. Katharine's Docks.
7. Guy's Hospital.
8. Star Music Hall.
9. Bermondsey Settlement.
10. Herold's Institute.
11. Rotherhithe Parish Church.

. Rotherhithe Hippodrome.
. Surrey Commercial Docks.
. Royal Victualling Yard.
. Foreign Cattle Market.

72.   One of the main tourist attractions in
London is Tower Bridge which dates from
1894; the approach road along which car 564
is travelling, was opened later and the electric
tramway service began in September 1904.
(C.G.Stevens)

73. Unfortunately the trams were never allowed to cross Tower Bridge and enter the City of London. Note the solid looking trackwork on the curve into Tooley Street, these eastern curves were installed in 1923 when the original western curves were removed. (R.J.S.Wiseman)

| UTE **68** | Greenwich - Surrey Docks - Bermondsey -- Waterloo Station | | | | | | | | | | | | | | P.M. times are in heavy figures |

Greenwich Church Street, Bridge Street, Creek Road, Evelyn Street, Lower Road, Jamaica Road, Parkers Row, Tooley Street, Tower Bridge Road,
w Kent Road, London Road, Waterloo Road

ILWAY STATIONS SERVED : Surrey Docks, Elephant and Castle, Waterloo

vice interval : MONDAY to FRIDAY 6 mins. (peak hours 5 mins., evening 8 mins.), SATURDAY 5-6 mins., SUNDAY morning 12 mins., afternoon
1 evening 8 mins.

	WEEKDAYS				SUNDAY					WEEKDAYS				SUNDAY		
	First	Last			First		Last			First	Last			First		Last
			SO	MF	•							MF	SO	•		
REENWICH *Church*	....	4 51	....	10 54	10 56	....	7 21	8 11	10 55	WATERLOO *Station*	5 12	....	11 30	11 30	7 25	8 0	8 47	11 30
rey Docks *Red Lion* ..	..	5 1	..	11 3	11 5	..	7 31	8 21	11 5	Elephant & Castle	5 16	..	11 33	11 35	7 29	8 4	8 51	11 34
wer Bridge	..	5 12	..	11 14	11 16	..	7 41	8 31	11 15	Old Kent Rd. *Bricklayers A.*	5 20	..	11 37	11 39	7 32	8 7	8 54	11 38
d Kent Rd. *Bricklayers A.*	5 2	5 17	..	11 19	11 21	7 16	7 45	8 35	11 19	Tower Bridge	5 25	..	11 42	11 44	7 36	8 11	8 58	11 42
phant & Castle	5 6	5 21	..	11 23	11 25	7 19	7 48	8 38	11 23	Surrey Docks *Red Lion* ...	5 36	..	11 53	11 55	7 46	8 21	9 8	11 52
ATERLOO *Station*	5 10	5 25	..	11 28	11 28	7 23	7 52	8 42	11 27	GREENWICH *Church*	5 46	....	12 2	12 4	7 56	8 31	9 18	12 2

SPECIAL EARLY JOURNEYS
w Cross to Waterloo Station, via Old Kent Road WEEKDAYS at 4 50, 5 0, 6 25, S0 6 37 a.m. ; SUNDAY at 7 3 a.m.

-Monday to Friday only. S0—Saturday only. *—Special Early Journeys.

7. Tooley Street to Greenwich

74.   Tooley Street terminus was a forgotten backwater, but tram service 70 had a mythology all of its own and rather belatedly it had a chapter to itself in a 1951 book, "London from the bus top" by Lucy Masterman. (R.J.S.Wiseman)

ROUTE 70	Greenwich - Surrey Docks - Bermondsey - London Bridge	P.M. times are in heavy figures

Via Greenwich Church Street, Creek Road, Evelyn Street, Lower Road, Jamaica Road, Parkers Row, Dockhead, Tooley Street

RAILWAY STATIONS SERVED: Surrey Docks, London Bridge

Service interval: MON. to FRI. 6 mins. (peak hours 5 mins., evening 8 mins.) SAT. 10 mins. (peak hours 5-6 mins.), SUNDAY morn. 12 mins., aft. and eve. 8 mins.

	WEEKDAYS		First	SUNDAY			
	First	Last	*	*	*		Last
GREENWICH Church	4 9	11 8	6 35	6 48	6 58	7 35	11 7
Surrey Docks Red Lion	4 19	11 17	6 45	6 58	7 8	7 45	11 17
Tower Bridge	4 30	11 28	6 55	7 8	7 18	7 55	11 27
LONDON BRIDGE Stn.	4 34	11 32	6 58	7 11	7 21	7 58	11 31

	WEEKDAYS			SUNDAY				
	First		Last	*	First		7 0	Last
LONDON BRIDGE Stn.		4 40	11 35				7 0	11 35
Tower Bridge	4 31	4 44	11 39	6 12	6 25	6 33	7 3	11 39
Surrey Docks Red Lion	4 42	4 55	11 50	6 22	6 35	6 43	7 13	11 49
GREENWICH Church	4 52	5 5	11 59	6 32	6 45	6 53	7 23	11 59

*—Special Early Journey.

SPECIAL JOURNEYS

New Cross Gate to Elephant and Castle, via Old Kent Road and New Kent Road, MON. to FRI. at 4 4, 6 20, 6 35 a.m.; SATURDAY at 4 4, 6 22, 6 34 a.m.; SUNDAY at 5 45, 5 59 p.m.

New Cross Gate to London Bridge, via Old Kent Road and Tower Bridge Road, SUNDAY at 6 56, 7 10, 7 23 a.m.

New Cross Gate to Tower Bridge, via Old Kent Road and Tower Bridge Road, SUNDAY at 6 15 a.m.

Elephant and Castle to Tower Bridge, via New Kent Road and Tower Bridge Road, MON. to FRI. at 4 22, 6 37, 6 52 a.m.; SATURDAY at 4 22, 6 39, 6 51 a.m.; SUNDAY at 6 3, 6 16 a.m.

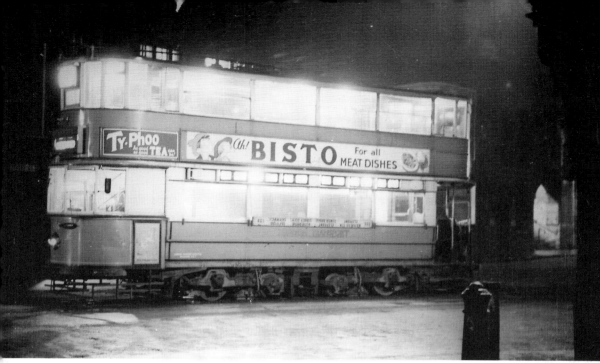

75. A welcoming sight to the weary traveller on a winter's evening is this tram, lights ablaze, getting ready to leave from Tooley Street. (C.Carter)

76. The Bridge Cafe is set into the retaining wall of London Bridge station. Passengers board car 595 which according to the indicator blind is only going a few hundred yards down the road! (C.Carter)

77. The terminus at Tooley Street handled the shunting of trailer cars on service 70 from August 1916 to April 1924, when the trailer experiment was given up by the LCC. Beyond the solitary tram in this view all has now been swept away in a redevelopment programme. (D.A.Thompson)

78. Car 556 is about to reverse by the Shipwrights Arms at the site of the former horse tramway terminus. (G.L.Gundry Coll.)

79. The parting of the ways for services 68 and 70; car 558 heads towards the terminus as a Brooke Bond Tea van crosses on Tower Bridge Road. The conductor has already altered the rear destination blind. (National Tramway Museum / H.B.Priestley)

80. The sharp bend at Dockhead by the Swan and Sugarloaf was part of local folklore and the squeal of the wheel flanges as they bit into the curve was a melody that lingered. (C.Carter)

81. Many buildings in this area had suffered extensive damage during the war and post war reconstruction left Dockhead high and dry as a new dual carriageway road was literally bulldozed through the neighbouring streets. All this is in the future as we observe car 554 picking up passengers in June 1951. (R.J.S.Wiseman)

82. Single track sections like this one along Parkers Row were one of the reasons why staff referred to services 68 and 70 as the slow road. Usually trams could only be driven at around half speed on these streets. Above the roof tops note the outline of the cranes serving the Upper Pool and St. Saviour's Dock. (Lens of Sutton)

83. The Parkers Row single track ended at Abbey Street, named after the former Bermonsey Abbey where Queen Catherine, widow of King Henry V retired in her old age. (John H.Meredith)

84. The next stretch of single line was opposite Wilson Grove in Jamaica Road. Derelict properties set the tone of this area; just before this spot on 10th May 1941 a whole row of houses nos. 123-169 Jamaica Road were flattened by a high explosive bomb. This view was taken on 10th June 1951 and the trams were abandoned exactly one month later. (John H.Meredith)

85. The reasons for the track layout can be appreciated as bus, tram and car fight for road space. The boy on the bike reminds us that in those days parents could allow their offspring more freedom to explore, safe in the knowledge that nothing serious would happen to them. (John C.Gillham)

P.&S. 2650   UNION ROAD, ROTHERHITHE.

86.   To cross from Drummond Road to Marigold Street in 1950 was merely a matter of a few steps over the granite setts and the tram lines. Subsequently the walk has been made harder by the insertion of a four lane highway at this point. (John H.Meredith)

87.   The postcard says Union Road, Rotherhithe and car 531 is pictured opposite Christ Church by Cathay Street. Union Road was later incorporated into Jamaica Road. (R.J.Harley Coll.)

88.   Three lads swagger along the pavement by the sorting office in Jamaica Road. The approaching tram is slowing down for yet another section of single line. Jamaica Road recalls the Jamaica House and Tea Gardens formerly situated in Cherry Garden Street and mentioned by Samuel Pepys in his diary in 1667. (D.A.Thompson)

89.   Car 561 lurches in the direction of the snack bar in Paradise Street. Staying with matters spiritual, notice the Norwegian Church of St. Olaf at the end of Jamaica Road, just by the entrance to Rotherhithe Tunnel. This fine 1927 church was designed by J.L.O. Dahl.   (John H.Meredith)

→

90.   The archway behind car 600 marks the entrance to Rotherhithe Tunnel; it is reputedly part of the cutting edge of the Greathead shield used to construct the tunnel which is a mile and a quarter in length and opened in 1908.   (R.J.S.Wiseman)

→

91.   The rivals pass on the bend into Lower Road; the 47 bus route has a long history and is still in operation. Note the marvellous street lamp to the left of car 595.   (D.A.Thompson)

92. On Lower Road by Surrey Docks station car 1566 slows to negotiate the crossover.
(John H.Meredith)

93. An 82 bus is about to cross the tram lines in front of car 556 which is halted at a temporary tram stop a few days before the abandonment of the service. The Surrey Commercial Docks were once a thriving place, steeped in history; here on the River Thames, Queen Elizabeth I went on board the Golden Hind to knight Sir Francis Drake.
(Lens of Sutton)

94. We are now in Evelyn Street at the bridge on which the former LBSCR goods only branch to Deptford Wharf passed over the single tram track. East of the bridge was situated Evelyn Street depot, which housed horse trams and then the LCC trailer cars. The building was vacated by the LCC in 1924.
(John H.Meredith)

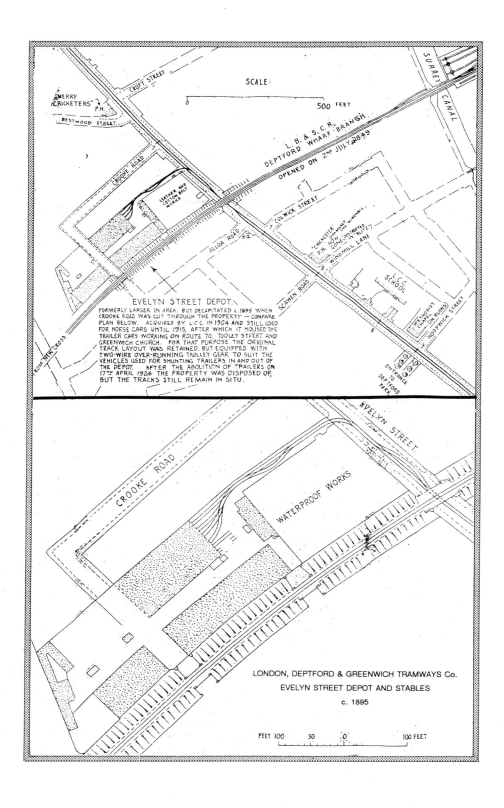

SCALE:

0   500 FEET

CROFT STREET

"MERRY CRICKETERS" P.H.

BESTWOOD STREET

CROOKE ROAD

L. B. & S. C. R.
DEPTFORD WHARF BRANCH
OPENED ON 2ND JULY 1849

SURREY CANAL

LEATHER AND COTTON BELT WORKS

COLWICK STREET

ALLOA ROAD   P.O.

"CRICKETERS" P.H. (FORMERLY WINDMILL) NOW DESTROYED — GONE IN BLITZ

WINDMILL LANE

L.C.C. SCHOOL

SCAWEN ROAD

METHODIST CHAPEL (IN RUINS)

HOPWICK STREET

KOM NEW CROSS

ENTRANCE TO DEPTFORD PARK

EVELYN STREET DEPOT.
FORMERLY LARGER IN AREA, BUT DECAPITATED c.1895 WHEN
CROOKE ROAD WAS CUT THROUGH THE PROPERTY — COMPARE
PLAN BELOW. ACQUIRED BY L.C.C. IN 1904 AND STILL USED
FOR HORSE CARS UNTIL 1915, AFTER WHICH IT HOUSED THE
TRAILER CARS WORKING ON ROUTE 70, TOOLEY STREET AND
GREENWICH CHURCH. FOR THAT PURPOSE THE ORIGINAL
TRACK LAYOUT WAS RETAINED, BUT EQUIPPED WITH
TWO-WIRE OVER-RUNNING TROLLEY GEAR TO SUIT THE
VEHICLES USED FOR SHUNTING TRAILERS IN AND OUT OF
THE DEPOT. AFTER THE ABOLITION OF TRAILERS ON
17TH APRIL 1924 THE PROPERTY WAS DISPOSED OF,
BUT THE TRACKS STILL REMAIN IN SITU.

CROOKE ROAD

EVELYN STREET

WATERPROOF WORKS

LONDON, DEPTFORD & GREENWICH TRAMWAYS Co.

EVELYN STREET DEPOT AND STABLES

c. 1895

FEET 100   50   0   100 FEET

95. Car 555 passes over the Surrey Canal at Blackhorse Bridge. The canal has now been drained and a large part of the former docks have been redeveloped into rather "up-market" housing; Surrey Docks station has been renamed Surrey Quays to fit in with this image! (D.Trevor Rowe)

96. The Black Horse at the corner of Hood Street and Evelyn Street provides the setting for this early horse tram view. There is a strong nautical tradition in these parts; John Evelyn and Samuel Pepys were both connected with the Admiralty and both fought hard for sailors' welfare. Peter the Great of Russia also came to Deptford to study shipbuilding. (J.H.Price Coll.)

97.   Creek Road, Deptford, by the Weslyan Central Hall and car 590 is eased gently through the curves by the traffic island. The Southern Electric sign points potential passengers along Deptford High Street to Deptford station the oldest in London. (John H.Meredith)

98.   We now have a view from the other side of the road junction. The pub on the corner behind the tram is the Noah's Ark, site of the original horse tramway terminus. (D.A.Thompson)

99.   A picture which typifies so much of early 1950s South London with the pub, the pollarded plane trees, the prefabs, the RACS milk float and the distant church spire. Car 572 proceeds at a leisurely pace along Creek Road, after having negotiated Creek Bridge. (D.A.Thompson)

100. Coming up to Creek Bridge car 1366 passes the blue RAC warning sign to encourage motorists to observe single line traffic on the temporary bridge ahead. (R.J.S.Wiseman)

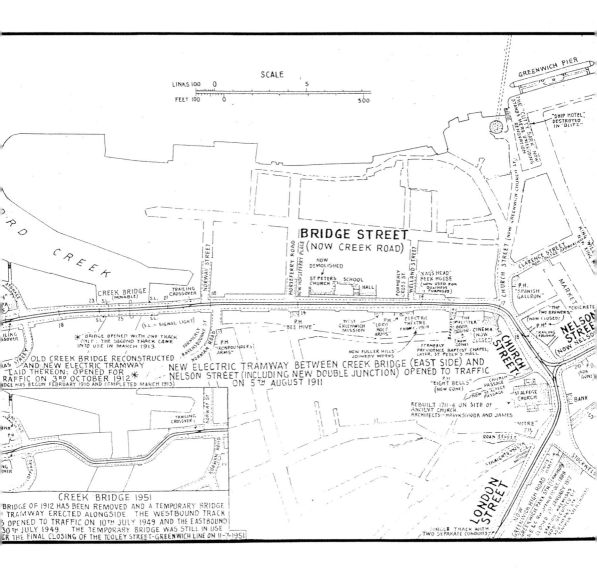

101. A rope has been drawn across the carriageway and an LCC motorman waits for the shipping to clear from Deptford Creek. Note the hatches in the conduit rails on the bridge, these could be opened to remove a defective plough or for a quick inspection of the T rails carrying the current under the roadway. (J.H.Price Coll.)

102. The original Creek Bridge with the
tramway was constructed in 1910-13.
Unfortunately for LT, because of the parlous
state of the structure, a replacement bridge
could not wait until sufficient buses became
available to supplant services 68 and 70. Work
began on the temporary bridge in 1949; this
and the following view show some of the
intricacies of conduit track construction.
(National Tramway Museum/ H.B.Priestley)

103. This shows the lifting section of the
temporary bridge and the photo was taken on
21st May 1949. (A.J.Watkins Coll.)

104. The new span is seen in use as car 572 trundles across; the westbound track opened on 10th July and the eastbound on 30th July 1949. (J.H.Price)

105. Up she rises! A rare photo shows the opening of the temporary bridge over Deptford Creek. (D.Trevor Rowe)

106. This is the Greenwich bank of the Creek. The notice for pedestrians seems to be an invitation to hitch a ride on a passing tramcar. The other warning sign by car 1529 is clear...Tramcars 5 m.p.h...Have Chain up...I presume this was to stop any short sighted passengers alighting in the middle of the Creek. (A.J.Watkins)

107. Looking towards Greenwich in June 1949 and the final days of the original bridge. As car 1089 crests the joining section in the roadway, the narrow shaft of the plough can clearly be seen under the tram. (National Tramway Museum / H.B.Priestley)

108. In the foreground the new tracks curve on to the temporary bridge and car 589 passes the end of Norway Street, a few minutes after leaving the Greenwich terminus. (D.A.Thompson)

109. The terminus in Church Street, Greenwich and a short break for the crew of car 1847 before the return trip to Waterloo. (A.J.Watkins)

110. Car 600 waits its turn before using the crossover in Church Street; it is carrying a blue and white advert for Oakeys whose wares were advertised extensively on London tramcars. (C.Carter)

111. The end of our journey; for many readers it will have been a trip down memory lane and for others, too young to recall the tramway era in London, it will have been a voyage of the imagination. (D.A.Thompson)

8. Rolling Stock

CLASS A

The class A cars, numbered 1-100, were the mainstay of the inaugural LCC electric services to Clapham and Tooting. The first A class car actually took to the rails on a test run on 7th April, some five weeks before the opening ceremony performed on 15th May 1903 by HRH the Prince of Wales. As can be noted from the pictures, the original open top design of the cars, as delivered from the Electric Railway & Carriage Co. Ltd. of Preston, proved inadequate for the demands of Londoners and top covers were soon added. The cars ran on Brill 22E trucks with the plough carrier fixed next to the pony wheels on one of the bogies. Reversed stairs were later replaced to give the motorman a better forward view. Finally, some cars were equipped with a trolley pole so that they could work on through services to the suburbs. These A class cars were relieved of their duties by the LCC in 1929-31 and by this time the original purple lake and primrose livery had weathered to a deep brown and cream. Trucks and electrical parts were salvaged and many car bodies were sold as sheds or temporary accommodation on the new housing estates around Sidcup.

Car 50 in original condition.

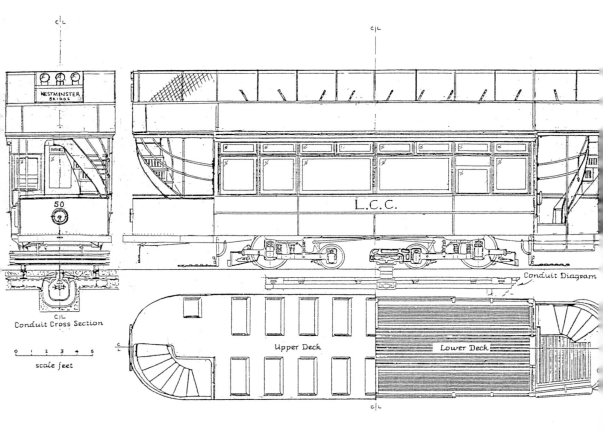

112. Car 86 was specially painted white for the
royal party at the opening ceremony.
(G.L.Gundry Coll.)

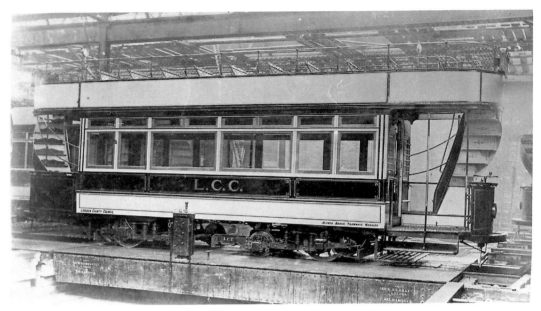

113. The handsome lines of the cars as built can be appreciated in this view of an A class tram on the depot traverser. (G.L.Gundry Coll.)

Car 20 in final condition.

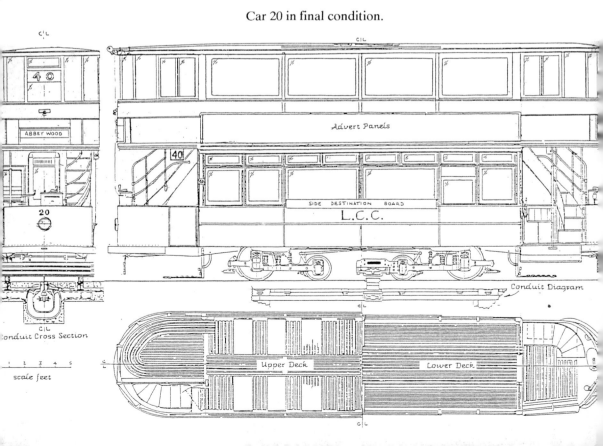

ABBEY WOOD

40

20

Advert Panels

SIDE DESTINATION BOARD

L.C.C.

Conduit Diagram

Conduit Cross Section

Upper Deck

Lower Deck

scale feet

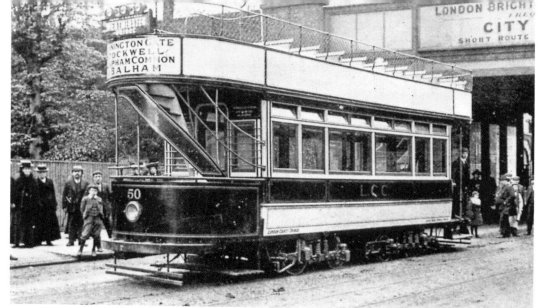

114. Out on the road in 1904 we can note the early indicator box topped with coloured lights to show the different services for those passengers who had reading difficulties. The painted destinations above the stairs were soon given up as impractical as more lines opened. (R.J.Harley Coll.)

115. The sumptuous decor of the royal car 86 with the sort of furniture that would fetch a fortune at an antiques shop today. Contemporary accounts describe the arm-chairs as upholstered in pale blue. The car was fitted with blue carpets and white curtains. (D.Jones Coll.)

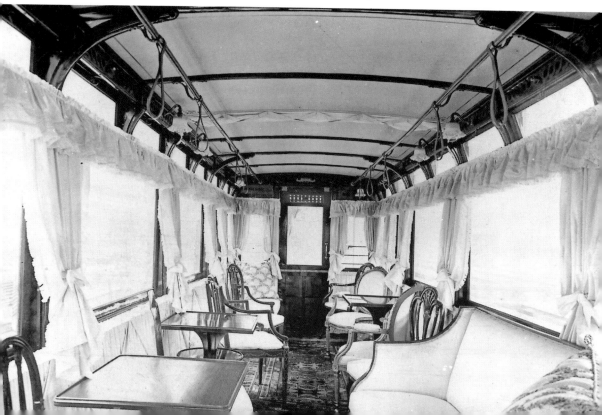

116. The more work-a-day atmosphere of a standard car with shaped plywood benches contrasts greatly with the royal car. (R.J.Harley Coll.)

117. The details of the whole car are revealed here; note the two stairs with viewing slots cut into them, also the bogie mounted plough carrier. (D.Jones Coll.)

118. This end view taken in May 1907 shows
car 52 as fitted with a top cover, but retaining
its reversed stairs. (D.Jones Coll.)

119. Just before being taken out of service, car 20 illustrates the final state of the class A car. This tram has been fitted with a trolley pole and direct stairs. (R.Elliott)

PETROL ELECTRIC

Three petrol-electric cars, numbered P1-3, were built as an experiment by the LCC. The thinking behind these trial cars was that they could take over from horse cars on some lines with light traffic, thus saving money on a full blown electrification of the route. Constructed in 1912-13, car P1 first ran in Woolwich; each car had a 40hp petrol engine which powered a generator which in turn supplied current for the traction motors. Cars P1 and P2 ran together on service 70 during the latter half of 1913, but the experiment was concluded in December of that year. Failure was due to overheating of the engine, noxious fumes and excessive noise. The three cars were converted into trailer tractor units and they finished their days shunting in Marius Road depot.

120. Car P1 is seen in 1913. Note the
"Mercedes" style radiator fitted in the left hand
dash and on the other platform can be seen the
petrol tank immediately above the engine
casing. (R.J.Harley Coll.)

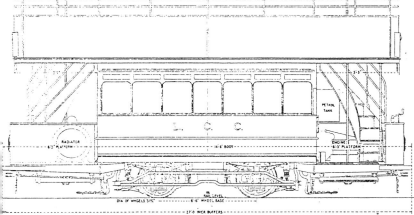

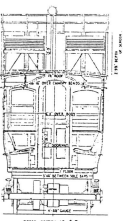